Simple Toys

Colin and Ann Carlson

Stobart Davies Ltd

Authors: Colin and Ann Carlson
Creations in Wood, Llanvaches, South Wales NP26 3AZ
Tel: 01633 400847 Fax: 01633 400847
www.creationsinwood.co.uk

British Library Cataloguing in Publication Data

A catalogue record of this book is available from the British Library

ISBN 978-0-85442-146-6

Front cover design: Betsan Evans

Published 2008 by
Stobart Davies Limited
Stobart House, Pontyclerc,
Penybanc Road, Ammanford,
Carmarthenshire SA18 3HP, UK
www.stobartdavies.com

Contents

When carrying out the projects shown in this book, to save destroying the book you may photocopy the plans, or use tracing paper to copy them.

All plans and text contained in this book have been carefully checked, however the authors and publishers accept no responsibility for errors and omissions.

Before starting, all instructions should be read and clearly understood.

Introduction

Having retired not long ago, we decided that we needed something to keep us occupied, and so we bought a couple of books on how to build toys.

The problem was that the toys shown were quite difficult to make and were a little too delicate for small children to play with.

With this in mind we decided to have a go ourselves.

This book contains the plans to make eight wooden toys, which are suitable for children of all ages to play with. We have fully detailed one of the projects, in a step by step way to try and show just how easy it can be, and have explained how to make these toys without the need of expensive tools and machinery. Page 4 includes a list of tools required to make the toys shown in the book.

Children's safety is of paramount importance, and when constructing toys they have to comply with European Legislation EN71. All the toys shown in this book do conform, however it is up to you to make sure when you are building them. Check all the glue joints are strong, by trying to pull them apart after the glue has had time to set and harden.

We prefer our toys to be left natural, however we have finished the helicopter on page 16 with some finishing oil to show you how that lifts the colours, and the wheels on the mini car have been painted blue. A lot of people like to paint them, so again be careful what paint you use. Paint which is suitable for children's toys will normally have a sign which says 'suitable for toys', if it doesn't then either check with the manufacturer, or find one that does. With regard to wheels, do what we do, buy them. Making wheels can be a very slow process, why go to all the hassle? We buy all our wheels and axles, so if you want them just contact us, the details are shown on the inside of the back cover.

We hope you enjoy making these toys as much as we have, and if you decide, like we did, that you would like to go into toy making in a more serious fashion, then why don't you contact The British Toy Makers Guild (details on the back cover), which is run by people like you who enjoy making toys. They have a range of booklets to help you on marketing and toy safety issues.

Tools

When following these plans you will need as a minimum the following tools:

Saw
Rule
Clamp – at least 1 (2 or 3 would be better)
Pencil
Adhesive (a good wood adhesive which should be waterproof, PVA or similar)
Drill
Selection of drill bits –
    6mm ($\frac{1}{4}$ in)
    9mm ($\frac{5}{16}$ in)
    10mm ($\frac{3}{8}$ in)
    15mm ($\frac{19}{32}$ in)
Sandpaper
several grades –
    rough about 40 or 60 grit
    medium 120 grit
    fine 200 or 240 grit

Finally.......
the most important, a mug of tea or coffee!

One quick note whilst on the subject of tools, a fret or coping saw will not cost you a lot, and it is a very worth while investment. It makes some of the more complicated shapes much easier.

Finally, before you start, a few words about wood:

Firstly you can use any wood you desire, but be aware of the following:

Price – which is self explanatory.

Ease of use – If the wood you choose is too hard it can be very difficult to work. Beech and birch are two of the toy makers favourites, we also like idigbo and ash.

Availability – If you live near a good timber stockist then most are available, if not your local DIY will normally stock pine.

Compatibility with toy making – The only real consideration here is probably how easily the wood splinters? Hardwoods like beech and birch are fine, however, soft woods like pine can be a problem, but an easy way to overcome this is to finish the toy with either a varnish or a lacquer, which will help to give it a more resilient surface, (just make sure it is 'safe for toys'.

Small Lorry

Materials List			
Main body	260mm x 50mm x 44mm	10¼ in x 2 in x 1¾ in	1
Cab sides	89mm x 64mm x 10mm	3½ in x 2½ in x ⅜ in	2
Cab roof	90mm x 75mm x 10mm	3½ in x 3 in x ⅜ in	1
Base for back	140mm x 75mm x 10mm	5½ in x 3 in x ⅜ in	2
Sides for back	160mm x 50mm x 10mm	6¼ in x 2 in x ⅜ in	2
Ends for back	75mm x 50mm x 10mm	3 in x 2 in x ⅜ in	2
Steering wheel	25mm diameter	1 in diameter	1
Wheels	50mm diameter	2 in diameter	4
Axle pins	6mm or to suit wheels	¼ in or to suit wheels	6

Materials list

We discussed earlier the choice of wood, and here we use idigbo. For us it is easy to obtain, our local timber merchant carries it as standard, and it is an easy wood to work with. You can use any wood you want, and if you don't have a good timber merchant handy then go to your local DIY store and purcase some pine (it will do just fine). Bear in mind you are building a toy, the exact size is not critical, near enough is good enough, and you don't have to use the same wood for all the components. Sometimes different woods look quite good together.

You can either make the wheels and axle pins yourself, or cheat like we do and buy them. There are several companies who sell them, or contact us (details on the back cover).

The back

We start with the back of the truck, once built the adhesive needs to dry and we can be getting on with other things whilst this happens. You will need 1 x 140 mm (5½in)r x 75 mm (3in) x 10mm (⅜in) for the base: 2 x 160mm (6¼in) x 50mm (2in) x 10mm (⅜in) for the sides and 2 x 75mm (3in) x 50mm (2in) x 10mm (⅜in) for the ends. We find it quite handy to build this upside down using a piece of 41mm (1⅝in) wood as a support. Put the base on the scrap wood to hold it off the table (see figure 2), and then apply adhesive to both the long edges and position the sides and clamp it (see figure 3). Be careful to ensure the sides overlap by 10mm (⅜in) each end. Now set this aside whilst the adhesive goes off. Depending on the adhesive you have used this will vary considerably. We find with the adhesive we use that it is set enough to take the clamp off after about 2 hours, but this does depend a lot on the temperature (in the winter it will take longer). If in doubt, leave it overnight, you can get on with something else in the meantime. When you are ready to proceed check to make sure the 2 ends are a good fit. If they are too tight then sand them a little, if they are too loose then you have cut them too small, you can either hope that the clamp will hold them whilst the adhesive sets, or cut another set!

Materials

Spread some adhesive on both ends of the base and the sides where they meet the end panels, then put them together and clamp. Again put to one side and allow to set. After this has set the back is complete with the exception of finishing. For this you need sandpaper and patience. As with anything you do, the outcome will depend a lot on the finishing. It is very important to take your time and do this properly. Start with some rough paper, a 40 or 60 grit, and take off all the edges, now move to a medium paper, a 120 grit, and smooth some more and finally finish with some fine paper, a 240 grit. You have now finished the back, put it to one side and get on with the rest.

Figure 1

The body

For this you need the piece of 260mm (10¼in) x 50mm (2in) x 44mm (1¾in)). Start with the cut out for the cab. You can either mark this out with a compass and rule, or use something of the correct diameter to mark around (the adhesive bottle for instance, see figure 4), or you can trace it straight off the drawing on page 10. Once you have marked it out you now have to cut it. For those with a fret or scroll saw, no problem, for the rest of us HOW? Well actually its quite easy, using a standard saw you cut down from the top to the line about every 3 mm (⅛in) (see figure 5). If you then press the pieces together with your thumb they snap out (see figure 6). Then start sanding (see figure 7). Now its time to drill the holes for the axles. The size depends on which axles you are going to use. If you are going to use a piece of dowel as a through axle, then the hole should be about 1-2mm (¹⁄₁₆in) bigger than the dowel. If, like us, you are going to use axle pins then the hole should be about the same size as the pins (in our case 6mm (¼in)).

You can either mark out with a pencil and rule or trace off the drawing, but make sure you mark both sides of the block. If you drill straight through, the drill can wander and you will end up with holes that are not square. The best way is to drill half way through from one side (see figure 8), and then turn the block over and drill through from the other side, until both holes join.

Whilst you have the drill out, it is as well to drill all the other holes. In the top of the main body you will need a 6mm (¼in) hole for the hood ornament, and another at about 45 degrees in the cab for the steering wheel pin,

Figure 2

Figure 3

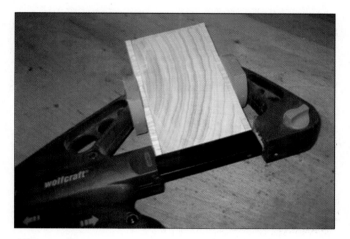

Figure 4

Figure 5

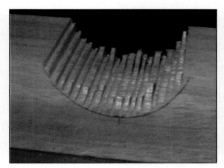

Figure 6

Figure 7

Figure 8

Figure 9

Figure 10

(see figure 9). Finally you need to drill out the centre of the wheels to suit whatever size axles you are going to use. The wheels normally come with the right size hole to suit the axle pins, but if you are using through dowel for the axles, then these holes need to be the same size as the dowel.

With all the holes drilled, it time to start taking off the corners of the body and adding a bit of personality to your lorry. There are several ways of doing this, for those with power sanders you can use them. If you don't have one you can take off the worst with a rasp or use rough sandpaper. Finish off by going through the different grades of paper until you get the desired finish.

Once the body is completed you can fit the steering wheel, whether it turns or not is entirely up to you. If you want it to, then make sure you drill the hole in the centre a little bigger than the 6mm (¼ in) pin. Push some adhesive into the 45 degree hole you drilled, making sure there is none left on the surface, and then push the pin through the wheel and into the body (see figure 10), and set to one side to allow it to harden.

The cab

For the sides of the cab you need the 2 pieces of 89mm (3½ in) x 64mm (2½ in) x 10mm (³⁄₈ in), and for the roof the 90mm (3½ in) x 75mm (3 in) x 10mm (³⁄₈ in). The first thing you have to do is mark out the windows (see figure 11). Again you can either use a pencil, compass and rule, or trace it straight off the drawing. To cut it out follow exactly the same procedure as you did for the cab (cut to the line every 3mm (¹⁄₈ in) or so, then push them together until they snap (see figure 12). Once the windows are cut out you need to take off all the corners with the sand paper, and get both sides really smooth.

Its now time to fit them to the side of the body. To do this you will need the clamp again. Place the body of the truck onto a flat surface, and put a little adhesive on to both sides where the cab will be. Now put the cab sides into position and clamp (see figure 13), ensuring you wipe off any excess adhesive with a damp cloth.

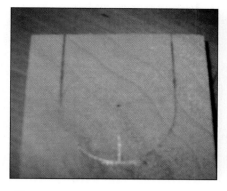

Figure 11

Figure 12

Figure 13

Whilst this is setting you can now start sanding the roof. Remove all the corners and give every edge a good radius, it does take a while but its worth it in the end.

The final assembly

Once the cab sides have set you can fix on the roof. Place a small spot of adhesive onto the top of each post, position the roof in place, longest edge side to side, and clamp (see figure 14), then allow to set. Then position and glue the back (see figure 15). Finally you need to fit the hood ornament, and the wheels. The hood ornament just needs a little adhesive into the hole, and then push it in. With the wheels, if you are using dowel axles, you should glue one wheel on to the end of the axle, then put it into place and glue on the other wheel (making sure no adhesive overspills onto the body). Repeat this for the other axle. If like us you are using axle pins, then first check their length, as they are normally fractionally too long, so you will need to trim about 12mm (½ in) off each one. Then put some adhesive into the holes, making sure there is none at all outside of the hole, and put the pin through the wheel and push it into place, repeating this for all 4 wheels.

You should now have a lorry similar to the picture shown below. We like to leave them natural, but if you want to paint, just make sure that the paint is safe for toys, and paint away. Its now time to start on the other plans in the book. Happy building.

Figure 14

Figure 15

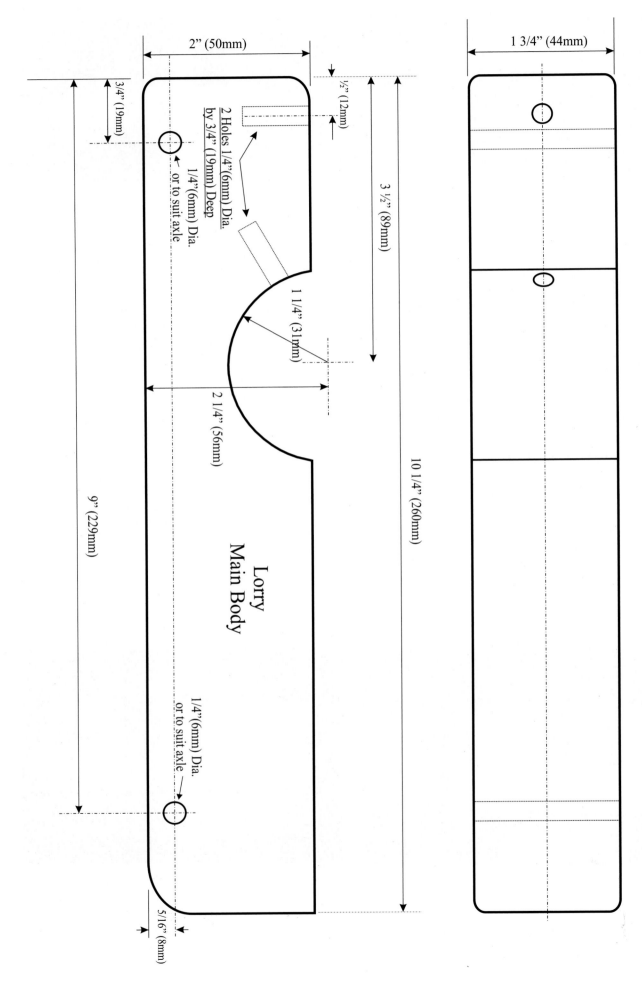

2" (50mm)

3/4" (19mm)

1/2" (12mm)

2 Holes 1/4"(6mm) Dia.
by 3/4" (19mm) Deep

1/4"(6mm) Dia.
or to suit axle

3 1/2" (89mm)

1 1/4" (31mm)

2 1/4" (56mm)

10 1/4" (260mm)

9" (229mm)

Lorry
Main Body

1/4"(6mm) Dia.
or to suit axle

5/16" (8mm)

1 3/4" (44mm)

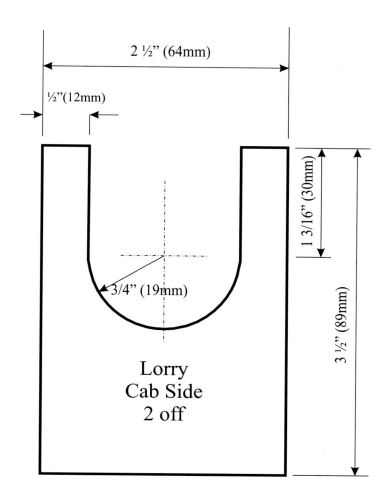

2 ½" (64mm)

½"(12mm)

1 3/16" (30mm)

3/4" (19mm)

3 ½" (89mm)

Lorry
Cab Side
2 off

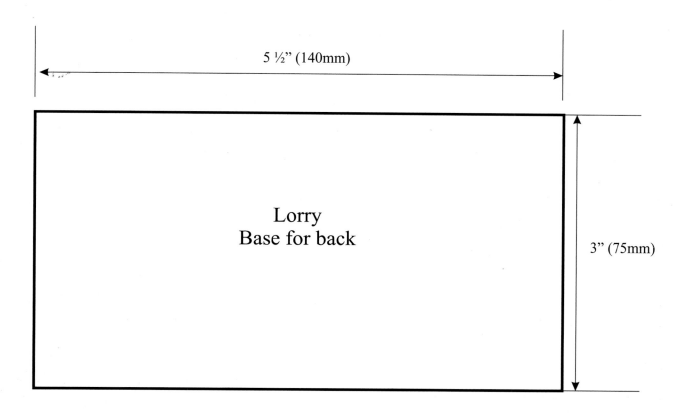

5 ½" (140mm)

Lorry
Base for back

3" (75mm)

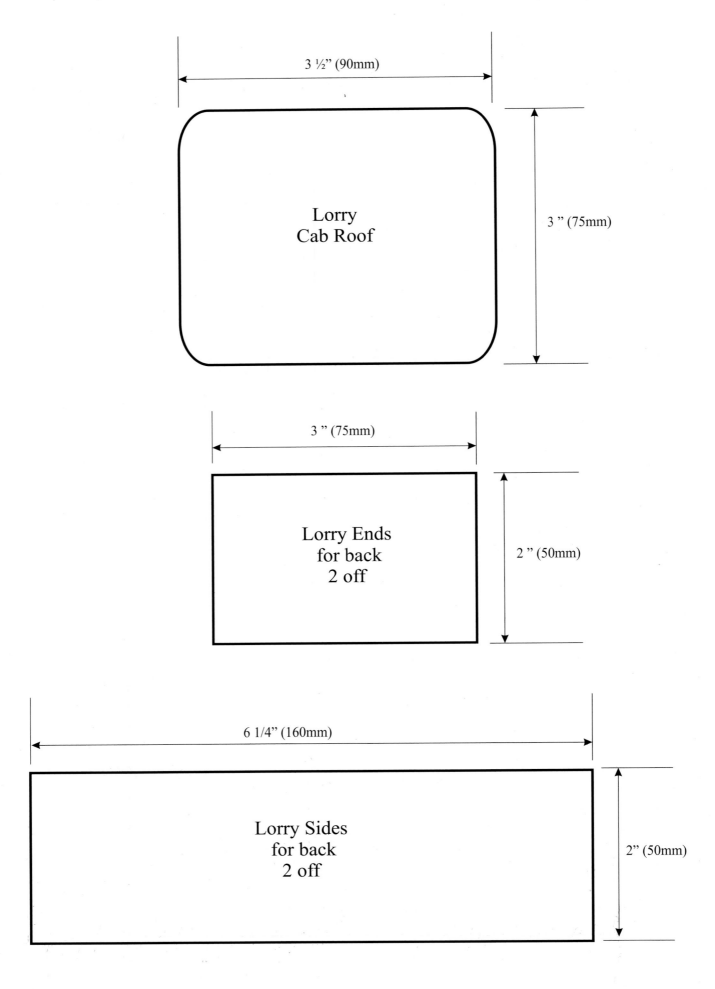

3 ½" (90mm)

Lorry
Cab Roof

3 " (75mm)

3 " (75mm)

Lorry Ends
for back
2 off

2 " (50mm)

6 1/4" (160mm)

Lorry Sides
for back
2 off

2" (50mm)

Small Artic

Notes

This lorry is almost identical to the first lorry. Build the trailer exactly as you did the back on the first lorry, and then you position the back axle in about the right place, (close enough is good enough). Glue the axle pin through the bed of the trailer, don't worry about the head sticking up into the back, its only small.

Materials List			
Main body	210mm x 50mm x 44mm	8¼ in x 2 in x 1¾ in	1
Cab sides	89mm x 64mm x 10mm	3½ in x 2½ in x ⅜ in	2
Cab roof	90mm x 75mm x 10mm	3½ in x 3 in x ⅜ in	1
Base for trailer	240mm x 65mm x 10mm	9½ in x 2½ in x ⅜ in	1
Sides for trailer	260mm x 44mm x 10mm	10¼ in x 1¾ in x ⅜ in	2
Ends for trailer	65mm x 44mm x 10mm	2½ in x 1¾ in x ⅜ in	2
Trailer axle back	50mm x 25mm x 44mm	2 in x 1 in x 1¾ in	1
Steering wheel	25mm diameter	1 in diameter	1
Wheels	60mm diameter	2 in diameter	6
Axle pins	6mm or to suit wheels	¼ in or to suit wheels	8

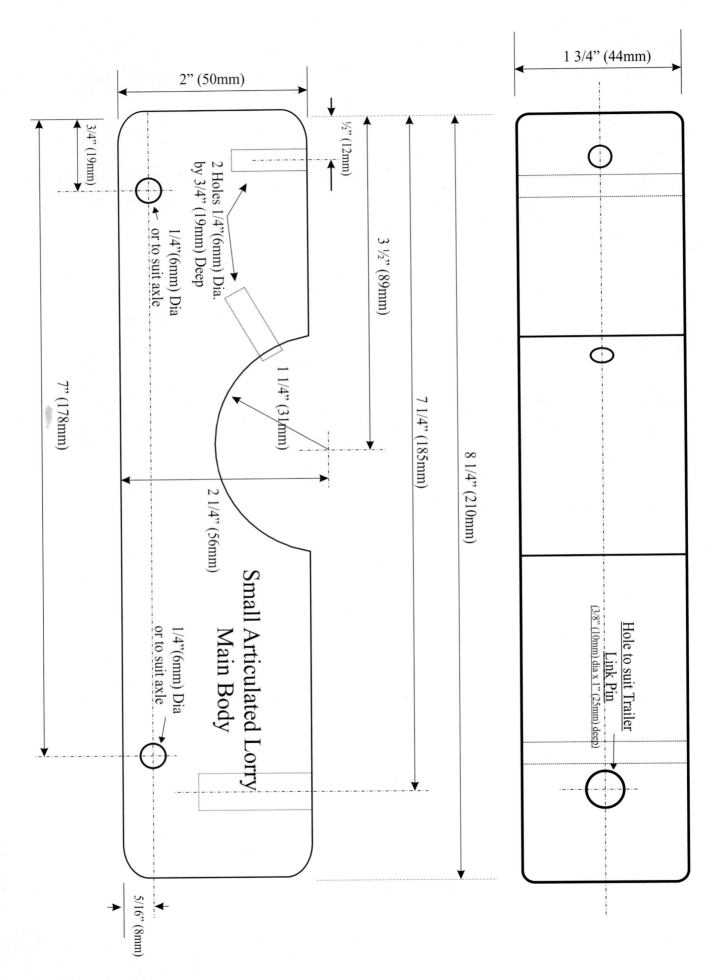

2" (50mm)

3/4" (19mm)

1/2" (12mm)

2 Holes 1/4"(6mm) Dia.
by 3/4" (19mm) Deep

1/4"(6mm) Dia
or to suit axle

3 1/2" (89mm)

7 1/4" (185mm)

8 1/4" (210mm)

1 1/4" (31mm)

7" (178mm)

2 1/4" (56mm)

Small Articulated Lorry
Main Body

1/4"(6mm) Dia
or to suit axle

5/16" (8mm)

1 3/4" (44mm)

Hole to suit Trailer
Link Pin
(3/8" (10mm) dia x 1" (25mm) deep)

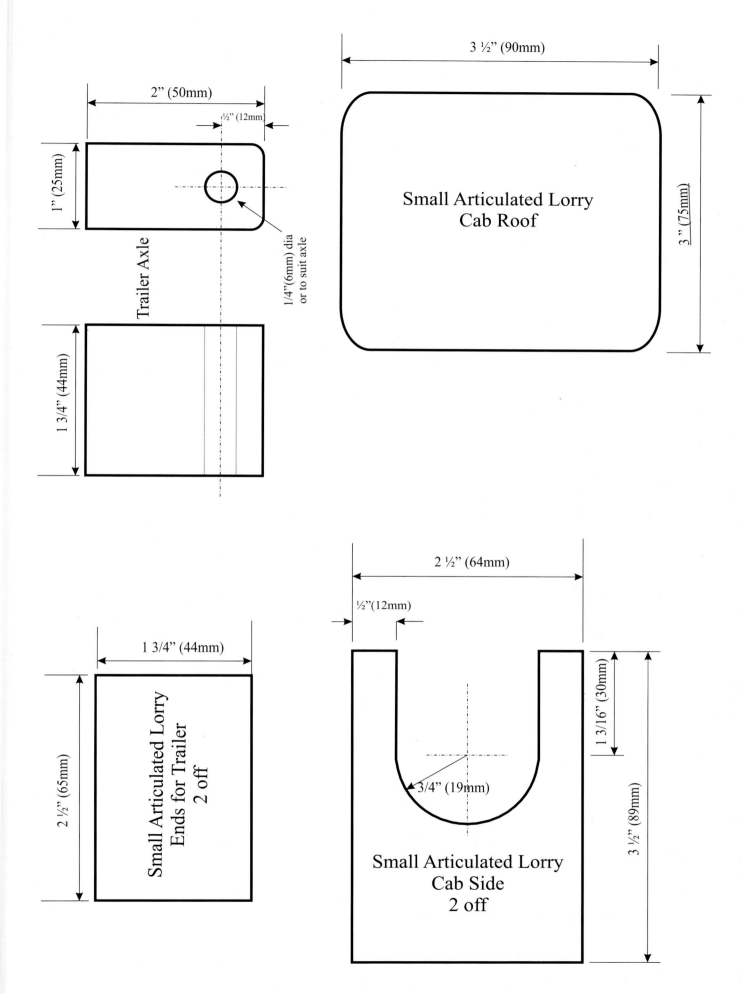

2" (50mm)

½" (12mm)

1" (25mm)

Trailer Axle

1/4"(6mm) dia
or to suit axle

1 3/4" (44mm)

3 ½" (90mm)

3" (75mm)

Small Articulated Lorry
Cab Roof

1 3/4" (44mm)

2 ½" (65mm)

Small Articulated Lorry
Ends for Trailer
2 off

2 ½" (64mm)

½"(12mm)

1 3/16" (30mm)

3/4" (19mm)

3 ½" (89mm)

Small Articulated Lorry
Cab Side
2 off

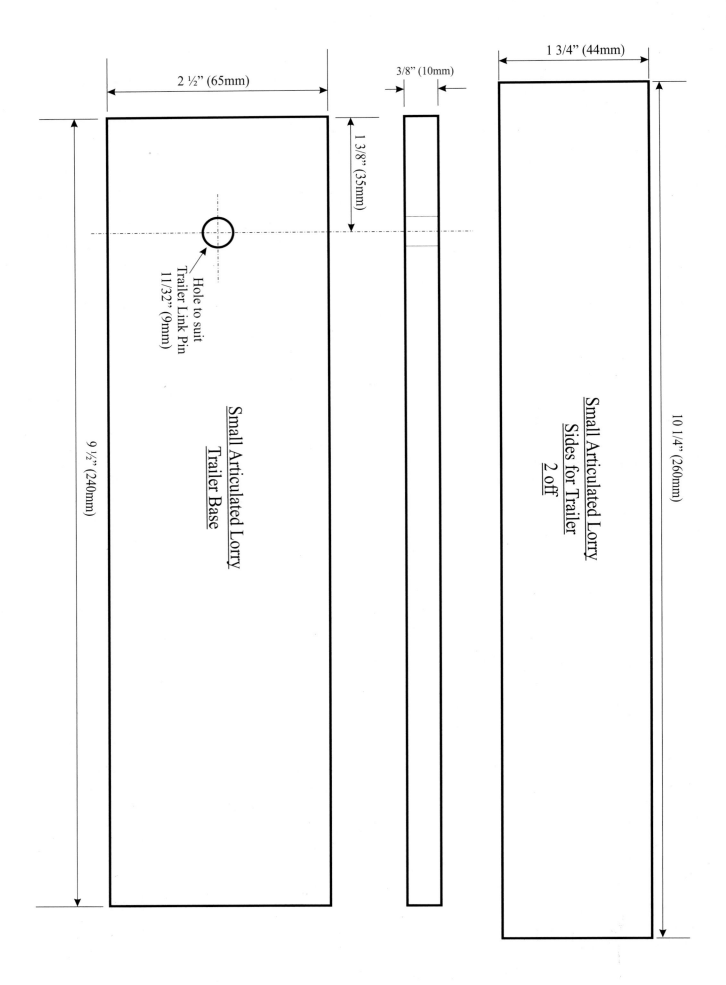

2 ½" (65mm)

3/8" (10mm)

1 3/4" (44mm)

1 3/8" (35mm)

Hole to suit
Trailer Link Pin
11/32" (9mm)

Small Articulated Lorry
Trailer Base

9 ½" (240mm)

Small Articulated Lorry
Sides for Trailer
2 off

10 1/4" (260mm)

Fire Engine

Notes

This lorry is almost identical to the first lorry. Make and glue the ladder together before cutting out the support, and then you can make the support width to suit, about 1.5mm (¹/₁₆ in) thinner than the internal width of the rungs. Push the swivel pins through the ladder and then glue them into the support, making sure that there is no glue residue outside the holes. Put the swivel pin through the ladder turn table, and then before gluing it into the support put a small steel washer over the pin and between the two pieces (it helps them to swivel). Finally glue the whole assembly onto the back of the body.

Materials List			
Main body	210mm x 50mm x 44mm	8¼ in x 2 in x 1¾ in	1
Cab sides	89mm x 64mm x 10mm	3½ in x 2½ in x ³/₈ in	2
Cab roof	90mm x 75mm x 10mm	3½ in x 3 in x ³/₈ in	1
Ladder turntable	100mm x 64mm x 12mm	4 in x 2½ in x ½ in	1
Sides for ladder	280mm x 12mm x 12mm	11 in x ½ in x ½ in	2
Ladder support	54mm x 33mm x 19mm	2⅛ in x 1⁵/₁₆ in x ¾ in	1
Ladder rungs	5mm x 46mm	³/₁₆ in x 1¹³/₁₆ in	10
Steering wheel	25mm diameter	1 in diameter	1
Wheels	50 mm diameter	2 in diameter	4
Axle/swivel pins	6mm or to suit	¼ in or to suit	8

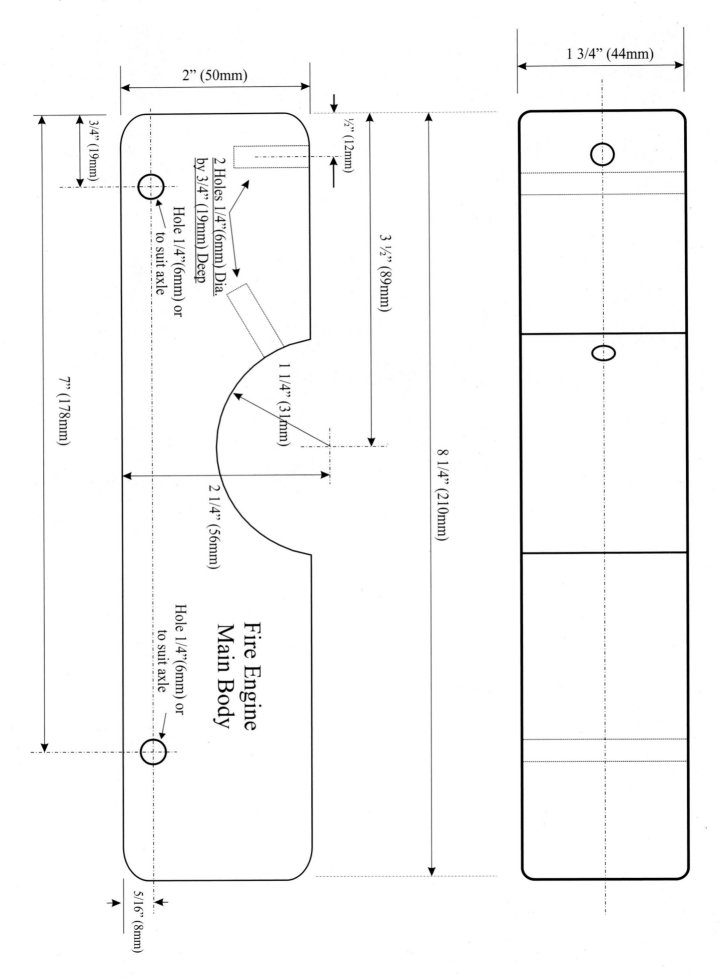

2" (50mm)

3/4" (19mm)

1/2" (12mm)

3 1/2" (89mm)

8 1/4" (210mm)

2 Holes 1/4"(6mm) Dia.
by 3/4" (19mm) Deep

Hole 1/4"(6mm) or
to suit axle

1 1/4" (31mm)

2 1/4" (56mm)

7" (178mm)

Hole 1/4"(6mm) or
to suit axle

Fire Engine
Main Body

5/16" (8mm)

1 3/4" (44mm)

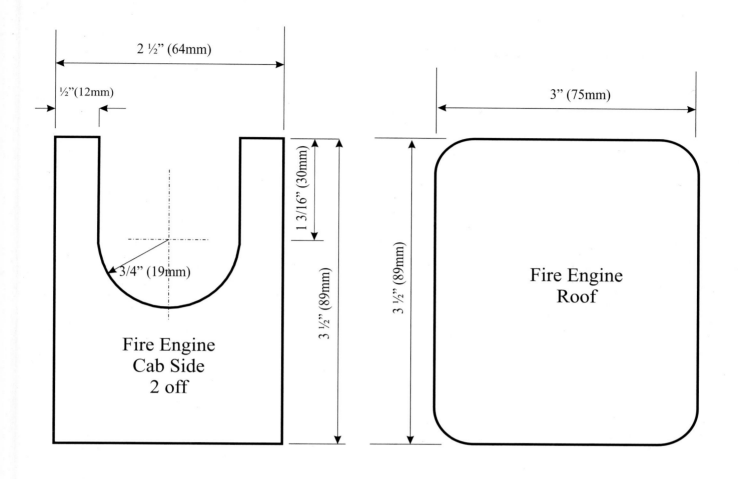

2 ½" (64mm)

½"(12mm)

1 3/16" (30mm)

3 ½" (89mm)

3/4" (19mm)

Fire Engine
Cab Side
2 off

3" (75mm)

3 ½" (89mm)

Fire Engine
Roof

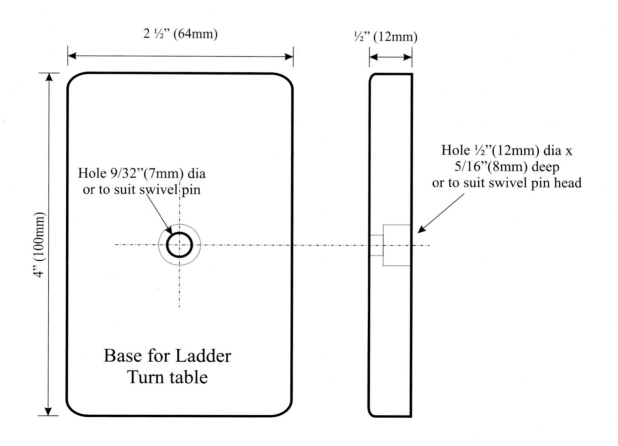

2 ½" (64mm)

½" (12mm)

Hole 9/32"(7mm) dia
or to suit swivel pin

Hole ½"(12mm) dia x
5/16"(8mm) deep
or to suit swivel pin head

4" (100mm)

Base for Ladder
Turn table

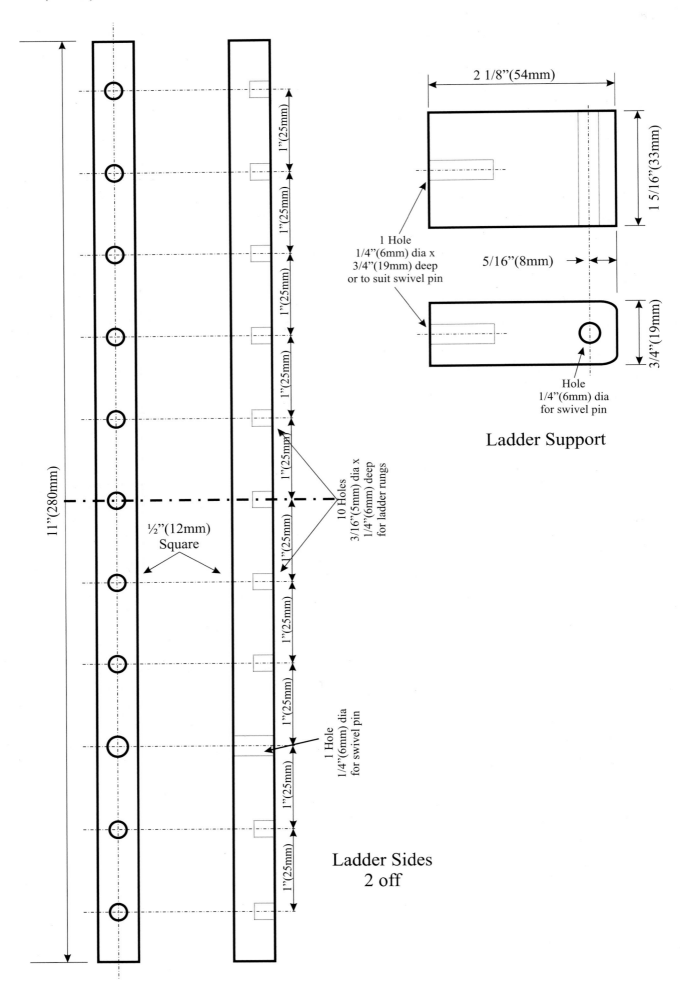

2 1/8"(54mm)

1 5/16"(33mm)

1 Hole
1/4"(6mm) dia x
3/4"(19mm) deep
or to suit swivel pin

5/16"(8mm)

3/4"(19mm)

Hole
1/4"(6mm) dia
for swivel pin

Ladder Support

11"(280mm)

1"(25mm)

½"(12mm)
Square

10 Holes
3/16"(5mm) dia x
1/4"(6mm) deep
for ladder rungs

1 Hole
1/4"(6mm) dia
for swivel pin

Ladder Sides
2 off

Tractor

Notes

The most important part of this toy is to make sure you round the corners off very well. It really makes it look very good, and gives a nice old fashioned look. For the exhaust I use one of the large axle pegs.

Materials List			
Main body	130mm x 44mm x 65mm	5¼ in x 1¾ in x 2½ in	1
Seat	40mm x 30mm x 30mm	1⁹⁄₁₆ in x 1¼ in x 1¼ in	1
Hitch	12mm dowel x 40mm	½ in dowel x 1⁹⁄₁₆ in	1
Hitch pin	6mm dowel x 17mm	¼ in dowel x ¹¹⁄₁₆ in	1
Steering wheel	25mm diameter	1 in diameter	1
Front wheels	50mm diameter	2 in diameter	2
Rear wheels	75mm diameter	3 in diameter	2
Small axle pins	6mm diameter	¼ in diameter	3
Large axle pins	9mm diameter	¹¹⁄₃₂ in diameter	3

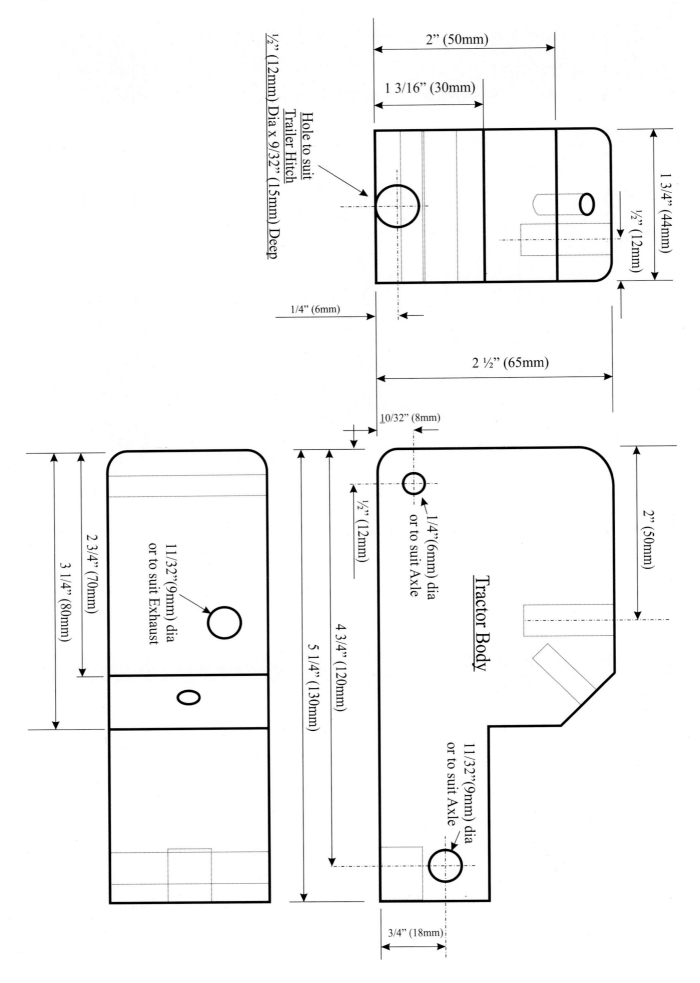

2" (50mm)

1 3/16" (30mm)

1 3/4" (44mm)

½" (12mm)

½" (12mm) Dia x 9/32" (15mm) Deep
Hole to suit
Trailer Hitch

1/4" (6mm)

2 ½" (65mm)

10/32" (8mm)

½" (12mm)

1/4"(6mm) dia
or to suit Axle

Tractor Body

2" (50mm)

4 3/4" (120mm)

5 1/4" (130mm)

11/32"(9mm) dia
or to suit Axle

3/4" (18mm)

11/32"(9mm) dia
or to suit Exhaust

2 3/4" (70mm)

3 1/4" (80mm)

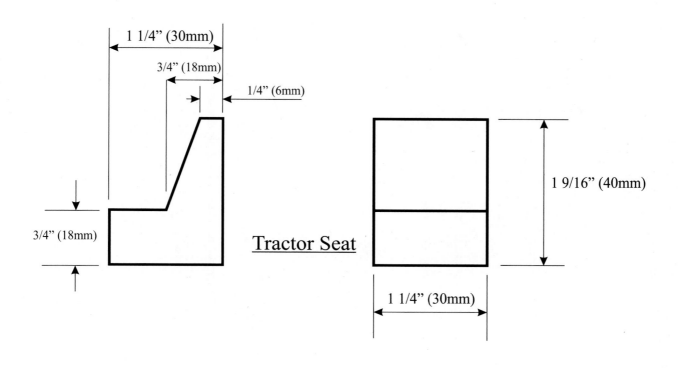

1 1/4" (30mm)

3/4" (18mm)

1/4" (6mm)

3/4" (18mm)

Tractor Seat

1 9/16" (40mm)

1 1/4" (30mm)

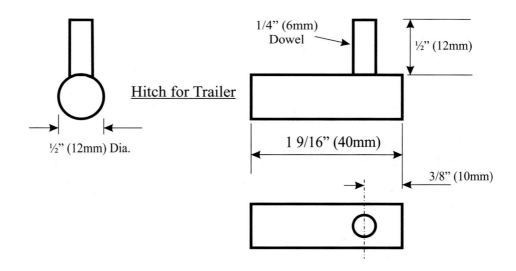

Hitch for Trailer

1/4" (6mm)
Dowel

½" (12mm)

½" (12mm) Dia.

1 9/16" (40mm)

3/8" (10mm)

Trailer

Notes

The construction of this trailer is very similar to the back of the lorry and the articulated lorry trailer. The only slightly difficult part is the linkage and to help there is a 3D sketch at the end the plans. By using the steel washer it helps the swivel.

It is also worth a mention that whilst this is designed for the tractor you could also make this fit the lorry by drilling the back of the lorry chassis and fitting a hitch, the same as the tractor's hitch.

Materials List			
Base	180mm x 75mm x 12mm	7 in x 3 in x ½ in	1
Sides	200mm x 44mm x 10mm	8 in x 1¾ in x ⅜ in	2
Ends	75mm x 44mm x 10mm	3 in x 1¾ in x ⅜ in	2
Axle supports	50mm x 44mm x 44mm	3 in x 1¾ in x 1¾ in	2
Link arm	12mm diameter x 100mm long	½ in diameter x 4 in long	1
Link arm supports	12mm diameter x 131mm long	½ in diameter x 1¼ in long	2
Wheels	75mm diameter	1½ in diameter	4
Axles	6mm diameter	¼ in diameter	5

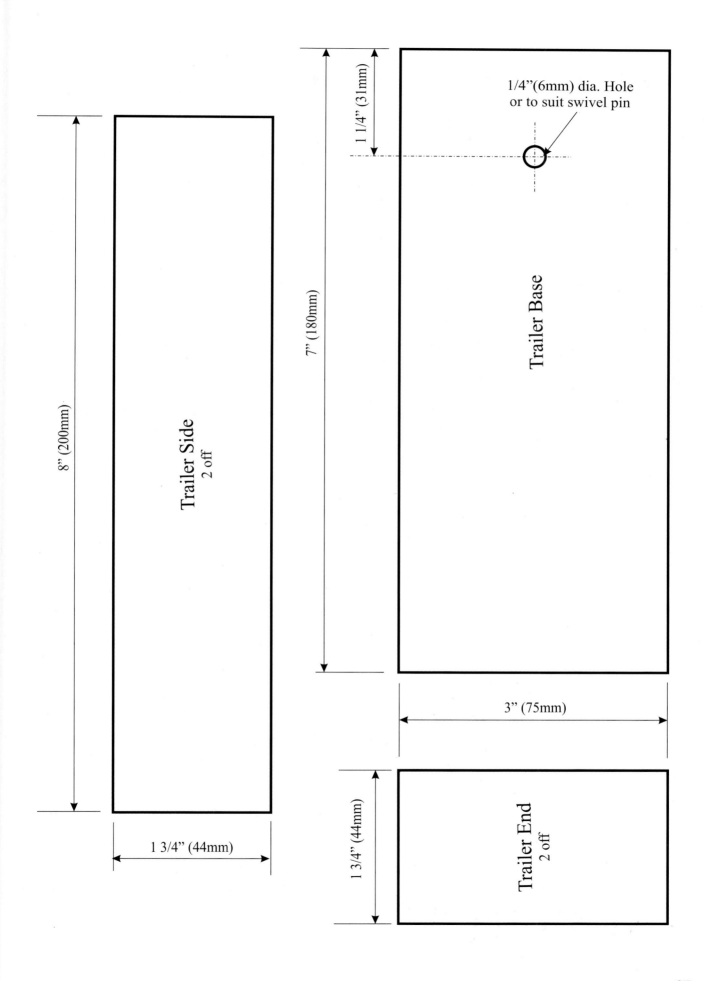

Trailer Side
2 off

8" (200mm)

1 3/4" (44mm)

1 1/4" (31mm)

1/4"(6mm) dia. Hole
or to suit swivel pin

7" (180mm)

Trailer Base

3" (75mm)

Trailer End
2 off

1 3/4" (44mm)

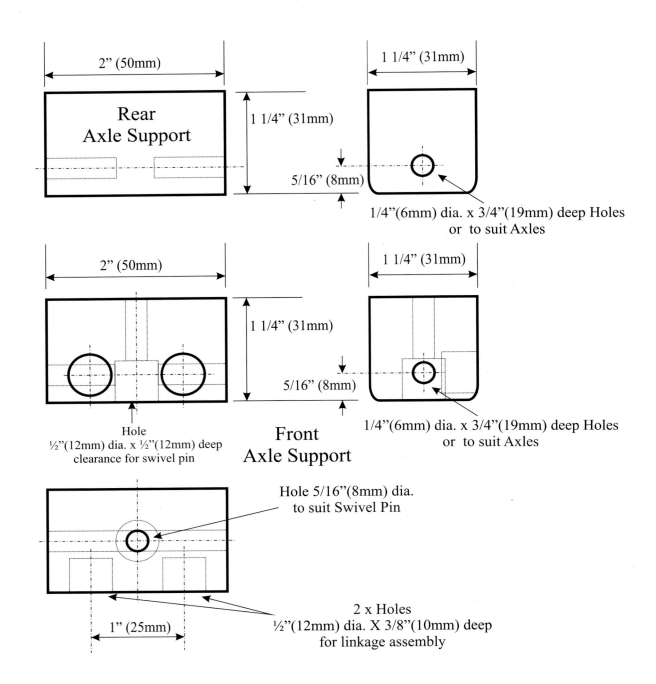

2" (50mm)

Rear
Axle Support

1 1/4" (31mm)

5/16" (8mm)

1 1/4" (31mm)

1/4"(6mm) dia. x 3/4"(19mm) deep Holes
or to suit Axles

2" (50mm)

1 1/4" (31mm)

5/16" (8mm)

1 1/4" (31mm)

Hole
½"(12mm) dia. x ½"(12mm) deep
clearance for swivel pin

Front
Axle Support

1/4"(6mm) dia. x 3/4"(19mm) deep Holes
or to suit Axles

Hole 5/16"(8mm) dia.
to suit Swivel Pin

2 x Holes
½"(12mm) dia. X 3/8"(10mm) deep
for linkage assembly

1" (25mm)

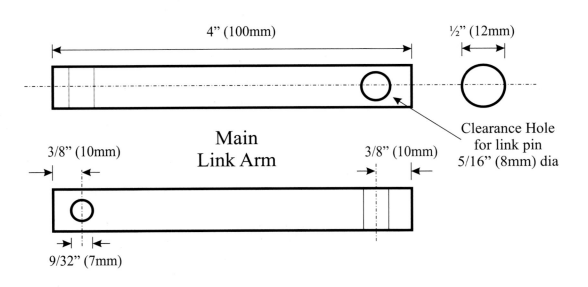

4" (100mm)

½" (12mm)

Main
Link Arm

Clearance Hole
for link pin
5/16" (8mm) dia

3/8" (10mm)

3/8" (10mm)

9/32" (7mm)

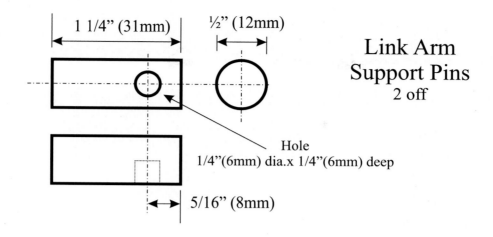

1 1/4" (31mm) ½" (12mm)

**Link Arm
Support Pins
2 off**

Hole
1/4"(6mm) dia.x 1/4"(6mm) deep

5/16" (8mm)

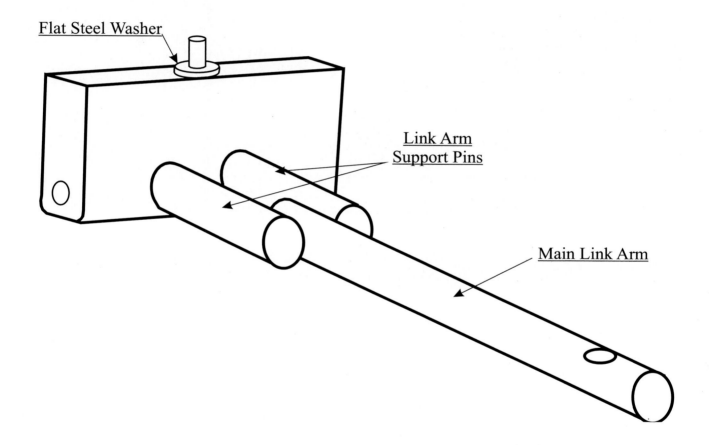

Flat Steel Washer

Link Arm
Support Pins

Main Link Arm

Trailer linkage final assembly

To finally assemble the trailer linkage, you should fit the main link arm to the support pins using 6mm (¼ in) dowel, making sure that the glue does not get onto the link arm, before gluing the support pins into the front axle support. When you fit the front axle support to the trailer, it is best to put a small flat steel washer over the swivel pin to separate the axle support from the trailer and this then reduces the friction and allows it to turn easier.

Aeroplane

Materials List

Main body	200mm x 75mm x 19mm	8 in x 3 in x ¾ in	1
Wings	180mm x 50mm x 10mm	7 in x 2 in x ⅜ in	1
Back wing	130mm x 50mm x 10mm	5½ in x 3 in x ⅜ in	1
Front	100mm x 19mm x 44mm	4 in x ¾ in x 1¾ in	1
Propeller	95mm x 95mm x 16mm	3¾ in x 3¾ in x ⅝ in	1
Wheels	45mm diameter	1¾ in diameter	2
Axle pins	6mm diameter	¼ in diameter	2
Pin for prop and skid	9mm diameter	¹¹/₃₂ in diameter	2
Dowel for wings	9mm diameter x 54 long	¹¹/₃₂ in diameter x 2⅛ in long	2
Dowel for fixing point	9mm diameter x 25 long	¹¹/₃₂ in diameter x 1in in long	2

Notes

If you have already built the first toys, then this one should be fairly straight forward. However, if you are starting off with this one, then you will need to consult the build instructions for the first lorry for tips on how to do certain jobs.

Begin by cutting out all the components before you start building. The most difficult is the propeller. You can do this by following the same basic idea used for cutting out the shape in the lorry body (see page 9), but if you took my advice earlier, and bought a fret or coping saw then this becomes very easy.

Start assembly by first gluing the wings into position on the body, with their two supports in place. Then assemble the front by fixing the propeller onto the front by placing the axle pin through the centre hole and gluing into the body, making sure there is no excess adhesive to prevent the propeller from turning, and do the same with the wheels.

Now fix the front to the body of the aeroplane by using the two 9mm x 25mm (11/32 in x 1in) dowel pins for location.

Finally, glue the back wing into its slot in the tail and cut an axle pin down by 20mm (3/4 in) (making it 25mm (1 in) overall length), and glue it into the rear of the body, as a back skid.

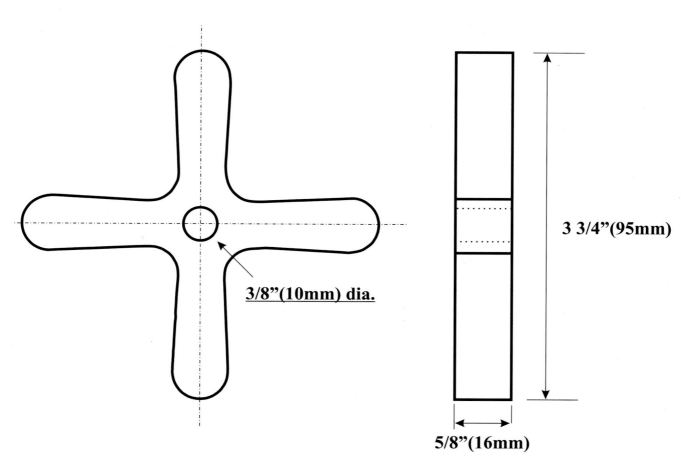

3/8"(10mm) dia.

3 3/4"(95mm)

5/8"(16mm)

Aeroplane Propeller &
Helicopter Rota Blade

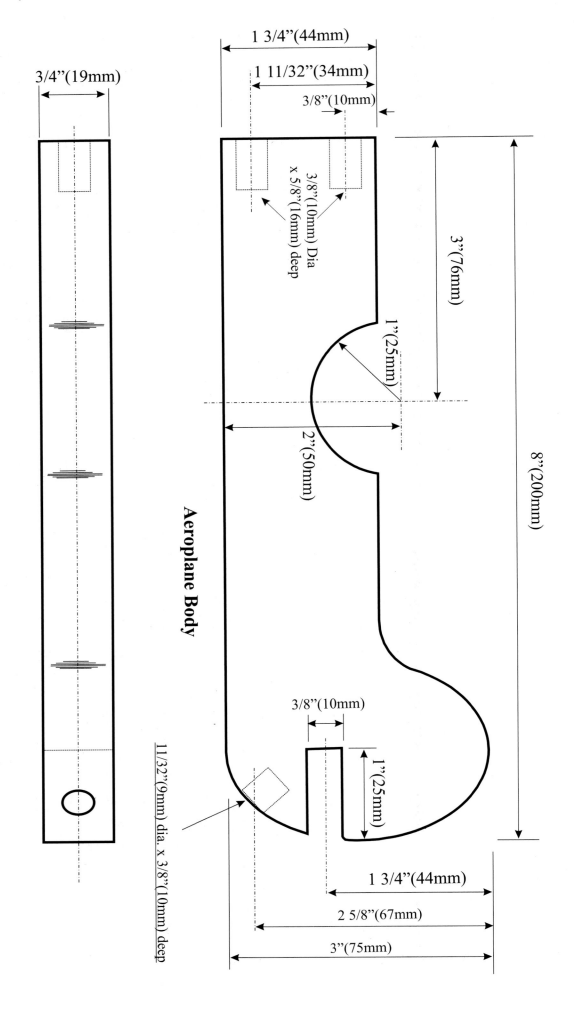

Aeroplane Body

3/4"(19mm)

1 3/4"(44mm)

1 11/32"(34mm)

3/8"(10mm)

3/8"(10mm) Dia
x 5/8"(16mm) deep

3"(76mm)

1"(25mm)

8"(200mm)

2"(50mm)

3/8"(10mm)

1"(25mm)

11/32"(9mm) dia. x 3/8"(10mm) deep

1 3/4"(44mm)

2 5/8"(67mm)

3"(75mm)

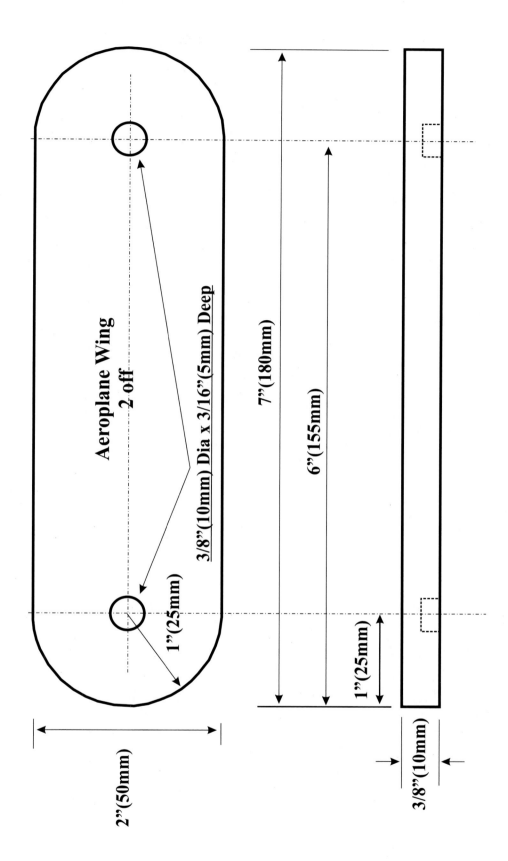

Aeroplane Wing
2 off

3/8"(10mm) Dia x 3/16"(5mm) Deep

1"(25mm)

7"(180mm)

6"(155mm)

1"(25mm)

2"(50mm)

3/8"(10mm)

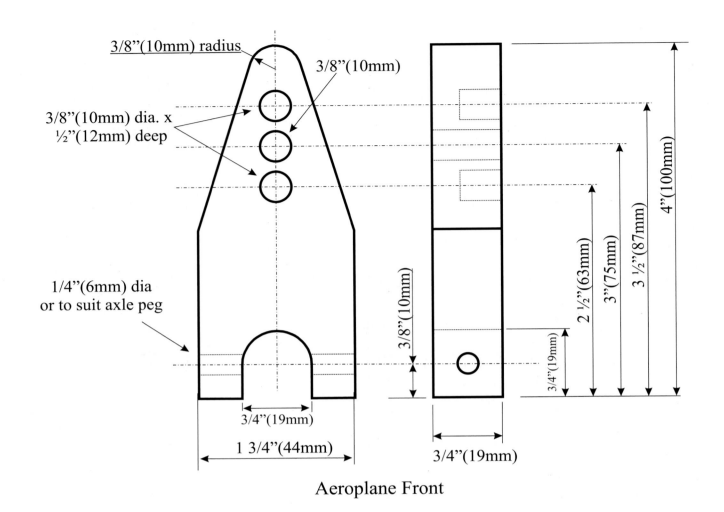

3/8"(10mm) radius

3/8"(10mm)

3/8"(10mm) dia. x
½"(12mm) deep

1/4"(6mm) dia
or to suit axle peg

3/8"(10mm)

3/4"(19mm)

2 ½"(63mm)

3"(75mm)

3 ½"(87mm)

4"(100mm)

3/4"(19mm)

1 3/4"(44mm)

3/4"(19mm)

Aeroplane Front

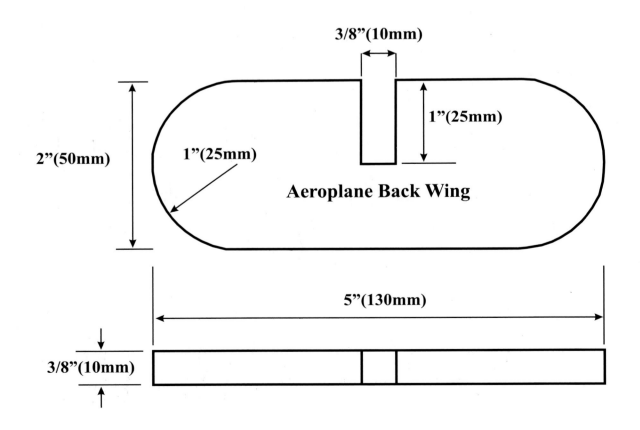

3/8"(10mm)

1"(25mm)

1"(25mm)

Aeroplane Back Wing

2"(50mm)

5"(130mm)

3/8"(10mm)

Helicopter

Materials List			
Main body	265mm x 85mm x 19mm	10½ in x 3⅜ in x ¾ in	1
Cab	75mm x 64mm x 19mm	3 in x 2½ in x ¾ in	2
Main rotor	200mm x 32mm x 19mm	8 in x 1¼ in x ¾ in	1
Back rotor	95mm x 95mm x 16mm	3¾ in x 3¾ in x ⅝ in	1
Floats	18mm diameter x 110mm long	¾ in diameter x 4⅜ in long	2
Float support arms	6mm diameter x 45mm long	¼ in diameter x 1¾ in long	4
Pin for rotors	9mm diameter	1¹¹⁄₃₂ in diameter	2

Notes

Once again, for this toy, begin by cutting out all the components before you start building. The parts are of a more difficult shape than the other toys, and here we really do recommend that you photocopy the drawings and trace them directly onto the wood.

To start assembly first glue the two cab sides to the main body. Make sure you get the sides the right way round. A tip for lining them up is to put a 19mm (¾ in) piece of dowel through the window, but make sure you take it out as soon as they are clamped,

otherwise you may get it stuck in there. The other idea is to fit the cab sides and drill the window after!

Next comes the two rotors. As with the aeroplane, make sure you don't push them in too far or it will stop them rotating. Make sure you don't use too much adhesive.

Finally, the floats are fitted with the 6mm (¼ in) dowel pins.

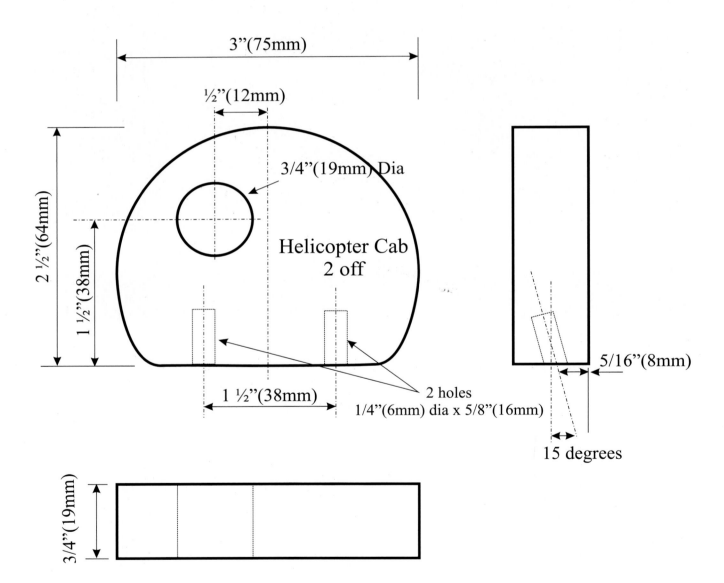

IMPORTANT:

The drawing shows the left hand cab. For the right side you must angle the two 6mm (¼ in) holes in the opposite direction.

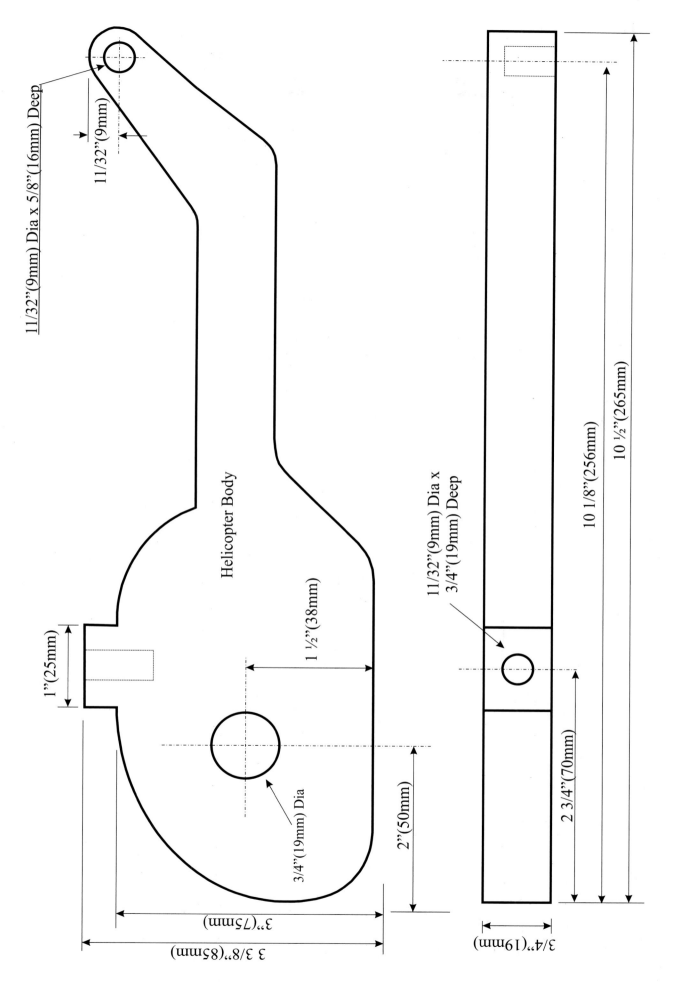

11/32"(9mm) Dia x 5/8"(16mm) Deep

11/32"(9mm)

Helicopter Body

1 ½"(38mm)

11/32"(9mm) Dia x
3/4"(19mm) Deep

1"(25mm)

3/4"(19mm) Dia

2"(50mm)

3"(75mm)

3 3/8"(85mm)

10 1/8"(256mm)

10 ½"(265mm)

2 3/4"(70mm)

3/4"(19mm)

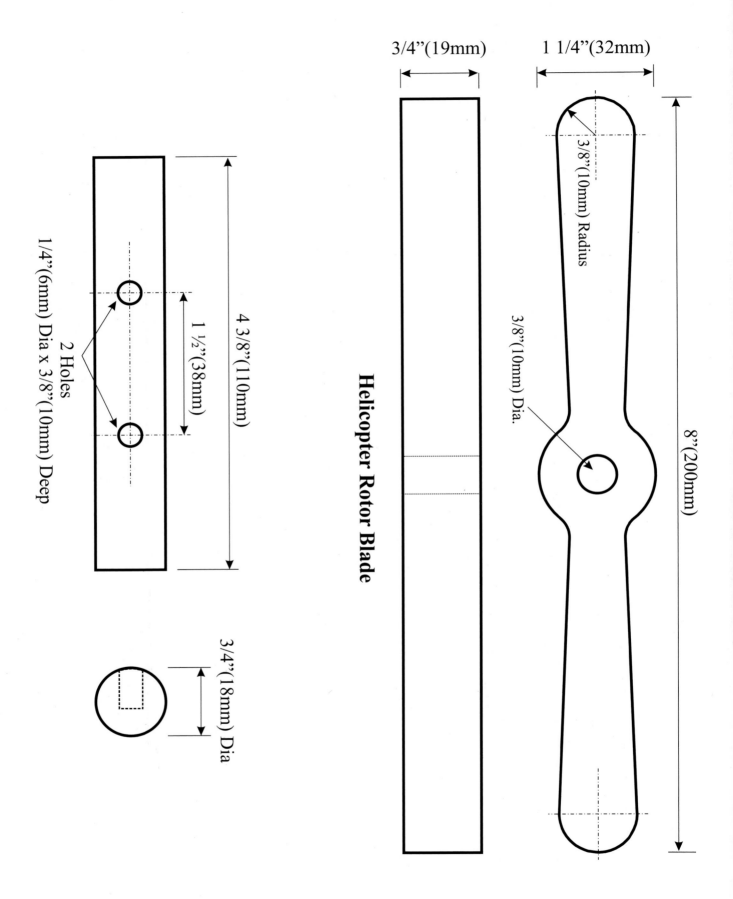

Helicopter Rotor Blade

3/4"(19mm)

1 1/4"(32mm)

3/8"(10mm) Radius

3/8"(10mm) Dia.

8"(200mm)

4 3/8"(110mm)

1 ½"(38mm)

2 Holes
1/4"(6mm) Dia x 3/8"(10mm) Deep

3/4"(18mm) Dia

Mini car

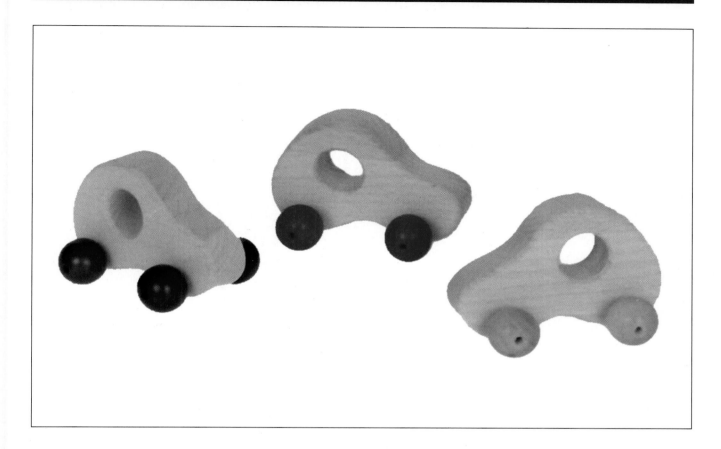

Notes

This toy really is the most difficult shape of all, so in this case do as I suggested with the helicopter, and just trace it straight onto the wood.

Materials List			
Main body	86mm x 57mm x 19mm	3³⁄₈ in x 2¹⁄₄ in x ³⁄₄ in	1
Wheels	19mm x diameter	³⁄₄ in diameter balls	4
Axles	6mm diameter x 38mm long	¹⁄₄ in diameter x 1¹⁄₂ in long	2

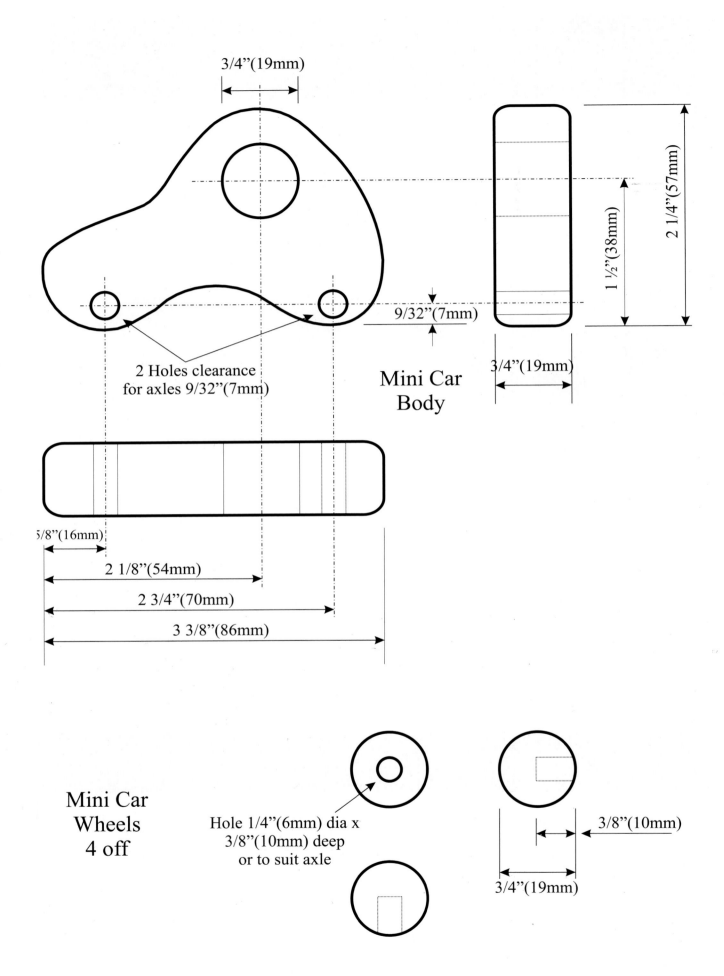

3/4"(19mm)

2 1/4"(57mm)

1 ½"(38mm)

9/32"(7mm)

2 Holes clearance
for axles 9/32"(7mm)

Mini Car
Body

3/4"(19mm)

5/8"(16mm)

2 1/8"(54mm)

2 3/4"(70mm)

3 3/8"(86mm)

Mini Car
Wheels
4 off

Hole 1/4"(6mm) dia x
3/8"(10mm) deep
or to suit axle

3/8"(10mm)

3/4"(19mm)